# The Intuitive Tarot Workbook

The first workbook that helps you develop an immediate Personal Intuitive Relationship with your Tarot Deck, Yourself, and The World!

## By Gina The Tarologist aka Gina Spriggs

# The Intuitive Tarot Workbook

# Table of Contents

# Introduction

Whether you are a new or an experienced tarot enthusiast, tarot study can be very confusing. No doubt you have purchased several tarot books and may even have a few decks. While some authors agree with each other, many do not. The result: An overwhelming feeling of confusion and skepticism. You may even find yourself asking, "Who should I believe?"

The answer is simple: ***Believe yourself.***

The hardest things to do is to learn tarot by rote. Memorizing and studying someone else's words of wisdom for 156 meanings (78 cards and all of their reversals) can be hard. As a self-professed late bloomer, my best lessons were learned by experience. I equate 'learning by experience' to when I was little and my mother gave me rule number one: "Don't touch the iron, its hot!" But I did touch the iron, and I nearly burned my fingertips off. And yes, I learned it was indeed hot. Rule number 546 from Mom: "Look both ways before you cross the street." I didn't listen until while crossing the street at age six, I almost got hit by a car. A friend once told me as a young adult, "Don't mix your liquor!" Well, *that* message fell on deaf ears until I experienced *the worst hangover ever* from drinking Long Island Iced Teas!

If you add to this confusion the number of decks that you own, you are almost guaranteed a number of mixed messages, and even more confusion.

I equate my tarot decks to people. Sounds crazy right? I know! The people I spend the most time with are my closest friends and family. They know me and I know them. My favorite decks are the decks I spend the most time with. Let me put it another way: I have 350 "friends" on Facebook, but whom do I rely on in an emergency? Who will always tell me the truth, no matter what? Who would I introduce to my mother?? Answer: Maybe 3 of my "measly" 350 FaceBook friends.

Still using the people metaphor – do you have any friends who share the same name? Are all Jennifer's alike? Many Gina's I know are short and Italian – *very unlike me.*

There are so many books on tarot card meanings, tarot origins, meanings of court cards, reversals, layouts, and the various methodologies to read tarot. This book is not one of them. Many of those books agree with each other, and many contradict each other. All of them are right for the author. I have my 'personal favorite' classics, and must admit to most recently appreciating those authors who encourage a more up-to-date, yet back-to-basics/personal relationship with your deck or decks.

There are two significant points of difference with *The Intuitive Tarot Workbook*. The first and simplest is the workspace provided therein. My biggest challenge over my years of study and practice has been reading a book on technique, and having to purchase a separate notebook for my notes, and trying to "keep it all together". I have several decks, and would use them all for my studies. I tend to "multi-task" and realize now what that means for me and others like me: The need for simplicity.

The second point of difference and most significant is addressing the intuitive approach to tarot. This, in my opinion, is the one most overlooked by students and teachers alike.

The most exciting aspect of this ignored approach is *the ease in practice and swiftness in which you see results.* There is no memory needed, no astrology knowledge required, and no real need to know how the elements relate to each other.

I want your studies to be as simple as possible while encouraging your journey with an accessible text *you can write in.* I created this book for a teaching environment, and then realized the potential opportunity to share the workbook itself. In my years of tarot study I have discovered the many techniques that work for me: Astrological references, Numerological references, and Intuitive references. There are many more – but these references unlock the key to the cards for me to give accurate readings. I do not purport that my current way of reading cards is the only way. On the contrary, I think the more one studies tarot, the more one's personal pathway is revealed.

I have learned to get to know my decks before I actually work with them. Similar to people, each deck has its own personality. I work with many decks, and own over 80. Each deck communicates in its own language, has its own accent, and speaks to me intuitively in a variety of ways. Just like you have taken the time to get to know your best friends on a one-on-one basis, I believe each deck deserves its own study. For example: the Morgan Greer Queen of Swords is a completely different person (for me) than the Hanson Roberts Queen of Swords. For me, any time I read someone using the Morgan Greer deck, and the Queen of Swords pops up, intuitively, I know that she is a warm person who either has a love of plants or has a first or last name that has to do with plants (like Heather, Ivy, or Rose). On the contrary, with the Hanson Roberts deck, I see a Virgo personality who is intelligent, and appears to be detached. No names pop up for me with this deck at all.

With that example in mind, my intention in creating this workbook is to help you gain a relationship with each deck you own. Each deck deserves its own study, and therefore its own workbook. (<u>Note</u>: To validate how the same cards in different decks can be interpreted differently, I will refer to several decks in this workbook – however, it is my belief that each deck you choose to study deserves its own workbook.)

*The Intuitive Tarot Workbook* is not something to add to your library of tarot cookbooks that offer card meanings and spreads. Focusing mostly on the intuitive process, this book will offer valued techniques to boost your intuition, precious tidbits based on wisdom I have learned from others, and tips and insights gained by my personal experience over the years. It will also offer more current study practices that allow you to gain insight into your deck's personality and most importantly, how you two will work together.

You will essentially write the "how to read my deck" portion yourself. The only requirement is that you have a deck you are interested in getting to know. My suggestion is that you select a deck with pictures on each pip card, also known as a pictorial tarot deck. The pictures will be the key to unlocking your intuition. You will gain, what I consider, *the most important key* to understanding tarot while using this workbook. You will learn to trust yourself, the deck you are studying, and your intuition. You will learn that the biggest difference between you and some of the world's most renowned and respected tarot scholars is the confidence they have in their craft. You will accept that your intuition is speaking directly to you, and trust in the most ridiculous thoughts that pop into your head while doing a reading. Finally, you will have done this with the help of a workbook that provides the assignments and blank space that allows you to document every step of your journey. Bon Voyage!

This book is dedicated to my

---

Tarot Deck

# Who Do You Think You Are?

Before we move forward with the real lessons, you have to take a test. Sounds odd, I know, to take a test before you actually learn anything…and that is the point. This is an "Answer truthfully because there are no right or wrong answers on this test". That's right, this is your book, and you answer only to you. The importance of this test is to allow you to identify your natural strengths so you can use them during readings. Using your innate strength, you will be able to naturally and easily give profoundly accurate readings without years and years and years of studying…(Yay!)

**Directions**: Circle the number that shows how strongly agree with the statement. Zero means you don't agree, and five indicates that you strongly agree.

1. When I watch movies and someone is being hurt, I feel the pain. 0 1 2 3 ④ 5
2. I often feel others emotions as if they are my own. 0 1 2 3 4 ⑤
3. I have "known" information based on no logical references. 0 1 2 3 ④ 5
4. I know which people in my life will get along with whom. 0 1 2 3 4 ⑤
5. I am often inspired with wisdom that I either write or share with others. ⓪ 1 2 3 4 5
6. I see vivid images in my mind's eye guiding regarding my future. 0 1 2 ③ 4 5
7. I feel as if I know how God would react in certain situations. ⓪ 1 2 3 4 5
8. I am confident that other worlds exist beyond this one. 0 ① 2 3 4 5
9. My friends describe me as an idealist. 0 1 2 ③ 4 5
10. I see signs in nature all the time. 0 1 2 3 4 ⑤
11. I can control the weather. 0 1 2 ③ 4 5
12. I can pick up an item and "read" the energy from it. 0 1 2 3 ④ 5
13. I know what someone is feeling even if they haven't mentioned anything. 0 1 2 3 4 ⑤
14. I feel things in my "gut" all the time. 0 1 2 3 4 ⑤
15. I know when someone is ill, and more importantly, what will help. 0 1 ② 3 ④ 5
16. I have heard messages that did not come from my mind. ⓪ 1 2 3 4 5
17. I have seen images of the future that came to fruition. 0 1 2 3 ④ 5

18. What would Jesus do? I know W.J.W.D!*       (0) 1  2  3  4  5
19. I like to learn about supernatural powers and the occult.       0  1 (2) 3  4  5
20. I feel like I can sense what is going on within someone's soul.       0  1  2  3  4 (5)
21. I am drawn to helping others with natural healing properties.       0  1  2  3  4 (5)
22. I can move traffic with the energy in my hands.       (0) 1  2  3  4  5

* *What Jesus Would Do*

Review the following statements and select the one that you relate most to with a five, and the others with a zero through four. Complete the following statement: *"If I could have one wish fulfilled, it would be...."*

| | | |
|---|---|---|
| 1. | To blink something into reality. | 0 1 2 ③ 4 5 |
| 2. | To remove the negative energies and feelings from others. | 0 1 2 ③ 4 5 |
| 3. | To obliterate racism and prejudice. | 0 1 2 3 4 ⑤ |
| 4. | To be in a relationship that exceeds my expectations. | 0 1 2 3 4 ⑤ |
| 5. | To hear Divine guidance whenever I need it. | 0 1 ② 3 4 5 |
| 6. | To clearly see all of my available options for the future. | 0 1 2 3 ④ 5 |
| 7. | To know in my heart what God wants in every situation. | ⓪ 1 2 3 4 5 |
| 8. | To access any available powers or energies to get anything done. | 0 ① 2 3 4 5 |
| 9. | To rid the world of poverty. | 0 1 2 3 4 ⑤ |
| 10. | To relieve the earth of harmful pollutants and chemicals. | 0 1 2 3 4 ⑤ |
| 11. | To use force to get things done, like creating things from thin air. | 0 1 2 3 ④ 5 |
| 12. | To be able to move objects to get things done. | 0 1 2 3 ④ 5 |

**Scoring Directions**: First, fill in the numbers you chose for each set of questions. Next, add up your points for each. All intuitive gifts are transferred to the body through the chakras. The following question sets correspond to one of the chakras and the gift associated with it. The chakras with the highest points house your strongest gifts.

| Questions | Total Points | Chakra | Psychic Gift |
|---|---|---|---|
| 1, 12, 23 | | One | Physical Intuitive |
| 2, 13, 24 | | Two | Emotional Intuitive |
| 3, 14, 25 | | Three | Mental Intuitive |
| 4, 15, 26 | | Four | Healing Intuitive |
| 5, 16, 27 | | Five | Spiritual Intuitive |
| 6, 17, 28 | | Six | Visual Intuitive |
| 7, 18, 29 | | Seven | Prophetic Intuitive |
| 8, 19, 30 | | Eight | Shamanic Intuitive |
| 9, 20, 31 | | Nine | Soul/Jungian Intuitive |
| 10, 21, 32 | | Ten | Natural Intuitive |
| 11, 22, 33 | | Eleven | Power Intuitive |

# Anatomy of a Psychic

As we embark on this journey, we are going to first take a really different view of ourselves. Who we "are" is not what just what we see in the mirror. We have seen and unseen energy that surrounds us and offers insight to where we have been and where we are going.

Chakras have a lot to do with our physical and spiritual existence. They act as receivers and transmission points for all types of energy. **Question:** Have you have ever woken up on a beautiful sunny day, ate a wonderful breakfast, said goodbye to your loved ones and made your journey to work… started your day off happy? Then on your way to work, you simply stopped to get coffee. When you arrived at work you realized that you suddenly were in a foul mood. What happened?

**Answer:** Just as we know we can catch a cold if someone who has a cold sneezes, (even though we may not be able to see the thousands of germ-filled spittle flying across the room aimed directly at our face), we can "catch" others energy. If you are around someone in a funky mood, you may just end up "catching" it! In this workbook we will learn to minimize the amount of energy we pick up from others, while identifying how chakras act as doorways for psychic information.

Healthy chakras are essential to our well-being and provide us with psychic feedback. I believe that focusing on our intuitive type is one way to develop the easiest relationship with your deck.

How do you discover your "type"? Below, I have elaborated on Intuitive types by Chakra. From there we will break it down into four essential types.

First, let's take a look at Intuitive Types by Chakra:

- **Physical Intuitive**: Chakra 1 – Physical Intuitives pick up sensations and/or illnesses that belong to someone else. An intuitive sense of smell is also found here. Many Physical Intuitives are good at Psychometry - the art of touching an item belonging to someone and "reading" it. I personally have found that, when this chakra is perfectly aligned and I am performing tarot readings, I pick up physical pains belonging to my querent. It is _always_ confirmed upon stating the pain. This chakra is located at the base of the spine.
- **Emotional Intuitive**: Chakra 2 – Unknowingly picking up emotions and moods from others, as described in the "sunny day" example above. Emotional Intuitive

are often described as "Empaths". In tarot readings, I clearly pick up the emotions of my client – especially fear or love. This chakra is located below the navel.

- **Mental Intuitive**: Chakra 3 – "Mental Sympathy" or the ability to "know" something even though there is no rational reasoning behind the knowledge. Due to the lack of physical sensations attached to this type of intuition, one often questions what they know. My advice: *Don't.* I recently had a reading with a woman and I sensed (and stated) a feeling of pending "gloom and doom" energy with her. She immediately denied it (and almost everything else I said). Then, later in the reading, she went back to it and explained that her husband of 37 years was terminally ill and she knew he was going to die. He refused to take the medication prescribed and would not go back for follow-up visits to his doctor. She told me she was "preparing herself" for his death. (Excuse me, but, if *that* is not gloom and doom, I don't know what is!). Upon reflection of this fact (and my poor choice of words) her reading made sense to both of us. This chakra is located in the ribcage.

- **Healing Intuitive**: Chakra 4 – Precognitive dreams, messages from guides during meditation, and healing energy are associated with the heart chakra. I once had a very detailed dream of a woman I didn't know. That day, I recalled the dream, went to my "Saturday Spot" where I do readings and noted that I was completely booked. However, a client with a one hour appointment canceled which allowed someone on my waiting list to take his place. The "replacement" was the woman I dreamt about, and my dream had a message specifically for her. This chakra is located at the heart.

- **Spiritual Intuitive**: Chakra 5 – Telepathy and transmediumship are associated with this chakra. I have to admit to a variety of "visits" that pop up during a reading. Many fathers who have transitioned speak to me and through me when I am doing readings.

On a more personal note, someone on the other side was making herself known to me because she could not get through to the person she really wanted to speak to. Throughout this time period, there were a variety of clues that made me aware that she was attempting to communicate with me. One of them had to do with The Star card in a tarot deck – "coincidently", her birthday was on November 17th, (17 being the number of The Star). She introduced herself in a dream, and let me know what her presence appeared to me as in my life. After she knew she had my attention she started harassing me just before sleep for days (she just would not stop talking!). She gave me the message, specifically for my friend, her intended recipient. She hung around for a period of time of which happened to be around the deceased and my birthdays. (I even have a picture of "her and I" taken in the last state she resided.). After that, she left me to live my life, and only makes infrequent appearances. This chakra is located at the throat.

- **Visual Intuitive**: Chakra 6 – Seeing images, metaphors, and pictures or "movies" that relate to the past, present, or future. This is where clairvoyance comes in. Before any of my appointments, I "take a clairvoyant peek" to see what I need to know. I am shown cards that always end up in my clients reading. This chakra is located between the brows.

- **Prophetic Intuitive**: Chakra 7 – Spiritual awakenings, prophecy and attunement to other worldly entities. A good example would be Edgar Cayce. I have found that (for me) certain cards speak directly of an Angelic presence – and *I am not* using a Doreen Virtue deck. This was something I learned in a meditative practice and I will share with you in this workbook. This chakra is located on top of the head.

- **Shamanic Intuitive**: Chakra 8 – Privy to present or past life information, these intuitives are often aware and operate with or through alternate reality portals. This chakra would be accessed when doing a past life reading. I had a reading where a woman asked about her relationship with a co-worker, who she felt very close to. Her reading revealed that, in a past life, her coworker was a nurse, and she was a wounded soldier. My client, Nancy, was a woman in her 50's and her co-worker in her late 20's to early 30's. The coworker continued (in this life) to be very attentive to Nancy and Nancy still felt eternally grateful. I find that people with this as their strongest chakra have access to the gifts of all chakras. This chakra is located an inch above the head.

- **Soul/Jungian Intuitive**: Chakra 9 – Many tarot enthusiasts are Jungian Intuitives. We identify and relate to archetypes and universal and/or individual symbolism when reading tarot cards. Often this "reality" is triggered when we first start our tarot journey because many books on tarot study reference Jungian psychology. This chakra is an arms length above the head.

- **Natural Intuitive**: Chakra 10 – This highly neglected chakra helps us breathe in the elements needed for both the physical and emotional body. These elements also aid in the health of our auric and chakric systems. We all need to be grounded. Intuitives and healers particularly need constant reinforcement to eliminate the waste or energies picked up by others in the healing process. Cyndi Dale mentions in *The Complete Book of Chakra Healing* that, when we are not grounded, we are susceptible to "physical and psychic attacks". She also goes on to say, "It is impossible to fulfill our life's mission without full assistance from this chakra…" (p. 77)… Personally, I have found that since I have discovered and utilized the "Psychic Tools" (which starts with grounding) my life and readings have enhanced greatly. This chakra is located about two feet beneath your feet.

- **Power Intuitive**: Chakra 11 – Many of these intuitive types use their hands to transmit the energetic properties of outside forces to provide raw energy to suit their purpose. What is ironic to me is that the gesture for "Speak to the hand!" utilizes this chakra and literally sends whatever energy coming to someone, back to the source.

  There is a thought process that speaks to all readings providing "healing" for both the readee and reader. That may often be true. You can determine the validity of that belief by how you feel (as readee or reader) *after* the reading. These chakras are located in the soles of your feet and palms of your hands.

When you review the list of intuitive types, there appears to be a slight sensitivity overlap. A simpler approach of identifying your Intuitive type is to lump them into four primary categories. They include:

- **Physical Intuitive**: Clairsentience – Those who interpret energy through feeling. Chakras one, ten, and eleven are "physical" chakras.
- **Mental Intuitive**: Clairvoyance – Those who see symbols, images, archetypes, and seek patterns. Chakras three, six, and nine are mental chakras.
- **Spiritual Intuitive**: Clairaudience – Those who hear messages from non-physical beings. Chakras five, seven, and eight are spiritual chakras.
- **Emotional Intuitive**: Empaths – Those who feel the emotions (stress, fear, happiness, or grief) of others. Chakras two and four are "emotional" chakras.

I like the four types because they specifically relate to tarot, as you will soon see. I bring you to know the eleven stated chakras for the purpose of being able to visualize perfectly *where they are and what their psychic function* is in your body. For a complete review of Chakras and all of their functions, I recommend reading any Cyndi Dale or Richard Gerber books on chakras.

*The next page is dedicated to the visual aspect of each chakra which may serve to aid in visualizing.*

To gain the confidence of knowing which chakra is where, review the placement of chakra and write it in. **Extra credit**: One chakra is missing. Identify it and draw it in.

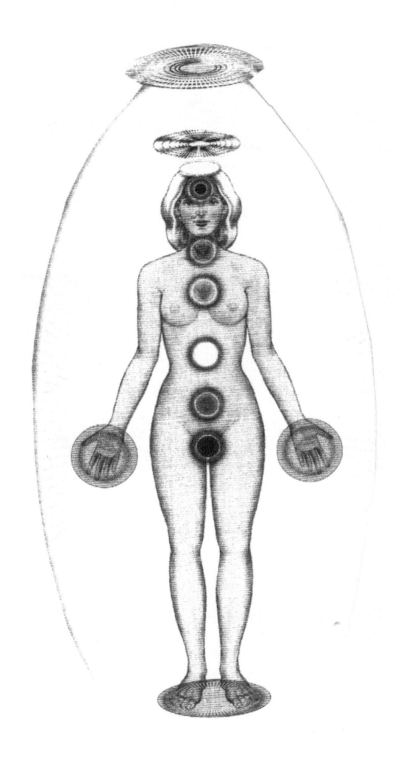

# Preliminary Exercises

Before and after doing any intuitive work, there are four key exercises that should be part of your regular routine:

- Grounding your environment and yourself.
- Protecting and separating yourself energetically.
- Charging your batteries and redistributing your energy.
- Calling upon/thanking the Divine for support while stating your intentions and anchoring

These four exercises create a firm foundation for you to draw on. In fact, whether I am doing intuitive work or not, I do these exercises daily.

**Note: Not only do these exercises help with harnessing your energy, these techniques are the foundation for building your intuition.**

## Grounding Your Environment

Your imagination is a very powerful tool. A term I like to use frequently is "I-magick-a-tion", because we first create our realities in our minds eye whether we know it or not. In Lynn McTaggart's book, *The Intention Experiment*, you learn in laymen's terms about quantum physics and how thought (or visualizing) is used to create real energetic change. Slow moving information being "quarks" – how most of us define reality and fast moving information being "tachyons" – which speaks to how we can pick up information intuitively. Most schools of clairvoyant study will require these techniques, although the order may be different. I mentored with Debra Katz, author of *You are Psychic*, *Extraordinary Psychic* and *Releasing the Genie Within*. Her techniques speak to Clairvoyance specifically; however, they go hand-in-hand with tarot intuition. These are practices referred to in her books and taught by her.

I first imagine that the space I am occupying (or where I am going) has gold columns of light in each corner of the room and in the center of the room. The columns of light travel down...past carpet (if the room is carpeted), wood, asphalt, different textures, colors, and temperatures of dirt, passing different life forms, until it reaches the center of the earth. I imagine the center of the earth being a pure non-polluted place abundant in its lushness of vegetation. I imagine that the grass there is thick, dense and a deep kelly green with golden dew sparkling on each blade. The colors are as vibrant as the energies they contain.  My columns plant themselves into the earth. Wherever I am or going, I imagine my name written all over the walls. My goal is to "own" the space energetically. Once I am confident that my space is grounded, I ground myself.

# Grounding Yourself

Sit in a chair with feet flat on the floor and palms up. Take a deep breath through your mouth, hold it for seven seconds and exhale through your mouth. Repeat at least three times. After you feel settled, imagine each of your primary physical energy centers (chakras), and the four outer body energy centers open, unblocked, shining at the same wattage, and spinning to the right. It helps to imagine each energy center on a dimmer while you adjust the brightness of its color. Go through each chakra by color: (Note: Those that can see auric fields will find that they rarely appear in this format, but this is the traditionally recognized color associations.)

1. Root Chakra – Red
2. Sacral Chakra – Orange
3. Solar Plexus Chakra – Yellow
4. Heart Chakra – Green
5. Throat Chakra – Blue
6. Third Eye Chakra – Purple
7. Crown Chakra – White
8. Eight Chakra - An inch above the head – Silver
9. Ninth Chakra - An arm's length above the head – Gold
10. Tenth Chakra - Two feet under the feet – Olive
11. Eleventh Chakra - Hands and feet – Pink

Once you have adjusted the wattage of each primary energy centers, return to your first and tenth chakras. Imagine that these chakras, located at the base of your spine and under your feet sprouts tails. The tails may be flesh colored at first. Your "tails", made from pure energy which may be coated with thoughts or worries, grow and penetrates the earth beneath you. It dumps physical and energetic worries (represented by the flesh) and as it approaches the pure center of the earth, it is vibrantly reflecting its pure natural colors. (I imagine green for my 10th chakra and red for my 1st chakra). Imagine that they literally plant themselves in the earth's center. Now, breathe in green and golden light from the earth. As this grounding energy bursts through lower body, it pushes out any residual unwanted energy left behind, and pushes up toward your head. You are now internally lit up 100% with green and golden light! I often get an all over tingling sensation when I do this exercise. Enjoy this feeling for a moment then push out 80% of the earth's energy from your feet. Retain 20% of what you took in.

You and your environment are now grounded.

## Protecting and Separating Yourself Energetically

Your aura is the reflection of your chakras. When chakras are healthy and balanced, so are our auras. The difference between psychic and intuitive styles is that psychics absorb outside energy into the body via a sympathetic mode that does not process energy. This can lead to illness and in extreme cases, death. The intuitive style is more empathetic, which involves recognizing and registering external energies then releasing, transforming or transmuting them.

My personal experience in the importance of grounding, protecting and separating before ***and after*** all intuitive work was a painful one… *Literally*. I was hired to do readings for a private party. The agreement was for two hours, but the day of the party, I received a call from the hostess advising me that I was an unexpected hit…(Why was she so surprised?), and that she expected I would probably be there for three hours. As it turned out, I was there for five hours, doing reading after reading. I tend to lose track of time in these situations, but when I came up for air, I realized the time and was asked to do one more reading. The lady who wanted the reading had been chatting with my partner all night, and both the hostess and my partner wanted me to read her, so I agreed. Unbeknownst to me, this beautiful, young, healthy looking woman had major issues with her heart chakra which were affecting her physically. The longer I sat in front of her, the more my chest hurt. After completing her reading (and advising her to go to a physician, ASAP!), I hurried to get my belongings, my paycheck, and my partner so I could start the fairly long drive home. As I drove I could feel the tightness in my chest swelling. I forgot to release her energy and reground – and she was coming home with me! It was so uncomfortable I vowed that would NEVER happen again!

That said, it is very important to be sure to ground your now balanced aura, by just imagining your rainbow colors reflected by your healthy chakras gathering under your feet and riding down your "tails" to the earth's pure center. Then, postulate your favorite flower or element rotating or surrounding your aura. I imagine a Sunflower or a ring of fire. This helps create distance, protection, and neutrality.

## Charging Your Batteries and Redistributing Your Energy

With all the movies and books now focused on Vampires, I must thankfully admit to have only been a victim of "Energy Vampires"- however, they can be just as bad. You know when you have experienced an Energy Vampire when after seeing them, or talking to them on the phone, they leave you feeling drained.

Your energy is your battery. Your best energy source is "you". When you find that you can't stop thinking of someone, or can't stop thinking about an event you would like to redo, you are literally scattering your energy, reducing your reserves. This next exercise will help you call it back, and works wonders!

While still seated and grounded, imagine you have your own personal sun, shining brightly over your head. Write your name in neon pink with orange trim or whatever colors you like. On top of your sun, is a disco ball, but instead of mirrors, it has shiny magnets. These two spheres shine brightly, the disco ball on top of the sun. Now, in your mind, hear your favorite song. Just because there is a cheesy disco ball over your head, doesn't mean your song has to be from the 80's! (My current favorite is Justin Timberlake "Bringing Sexy Back" – which I believe is well suited for this exercise!) As your song plays, you are feeling happy which lifts your vibration. Your scattered energy returns to you from the past, present, and future worries and concerns. It slaps thickly onto the disco ball. I imagine a textured substance like honey, slapping on the disco ball and sliding down, into my sun. Once there, it is boiled clean from the residue of where it has been. I imagine a screen-textured strainer at the bottom of my sun that sieves my cleansed energy, and leads to a trap door. Now, it is time to release your energy from your sun. The trap door opens and allows it to flow into your awaiting and open 9th, 8th and crown chakra. Here, due to the weight of our energy, it drops immediately to your feet, filling up the inside of your body quickly. As it approaches the top of your neck, it fills up your head and overflows from your mouth, ears, eyes, nose and crown chakra. You are now glistening, inside and out with your own energy! Keep these spheres above your head for a while. We will call on them in a bit.

# Redistributing Your Energy

This exercise is done prior to *and* after any intuitive activity. As a reminder, we set your primary energy centers to the same wattage. Well, now we want to call upon most of the energy from our bottom four chakras, and bring it up to our top chakras. While in our intuitive space, we will not need to call upon all of the survival energy from the root chakra, creative energy from our naval chakra, analytical energy from our solar plexus, or compassionate energy from our heart chakra.

We will need our throat chakra to share the information we are receiving from the universe, our third eye to access the information, and our crown, 8th and 9th chakras to receive it. This is a lot of work for these chakras, so we will borrow some energy for the purpose of doing intuitive work. (For those of you concerned, yes, you will still be compassionate and creative; however, you won't suddenly start sobbing when emotions are overflowing from your querent. You become objective, supportive, and most of all, neutral.)

Below is my personal process. I invite you to review it and take what resonates within you, while adjusting what you want.

I imagine an internal elevator opening its doors at my root chakra. Ninety percent of this powerful red energy gets on the elevator, the doors close and proceeds to move up to the navel chakra, where upon the doors open again an allows 90% of my bright orange energy to get on. The doors close and open again when it reaches my solar plexus. Ninety percent of this vibrant yellow energy gets on the elevator and the doors close again. When it moves up to my heart chakra, the doors open and allows 90% of the soothing green energy to slip in. At this point there is a beautiful rainbow of energy in the elevator! When it reaches the throat chakra, an amazing thing happens. A spiral staircase connects the last three energy centers, and there is a party going on. The elevator opens and a burst of energy pops out. The largest space seems to be the third eye level, in between the throat and crown, where a giant screen is in the middle of the room. There are soft, lush purple comfy couches right in front of the screen. Have a seat! On the screen, imagine a big eye. (My eye is Liz Taylor violet with silver sparkles!) It is through this eye that you will be "seeing" while in this intuitive space. On your left there is a remote control. It has two knobs. One says "Intuition" and controls the higher chakras. The other says "Analyzer", and controls your lower chakras. Turn up your intuition as far as it will go and turn down your analyzer.

# Calling Upon and Thanking the Divine for Support while Stating your Intentions

While you have been getting comfortable in your intuitive space, you've had two spheres hanging out over your head - your sun and disco ball. Imagine sending these two spheres up over your house, about 30,000 feet. Imagine they look back at you, see that your are fine...and continue out of your state, out of this planet, out of this solar system and stratosphere, into the universe where they meet the Divine. Once in front of this powerful source of energy, they burst into a billion trillion purple light and silver light particles that absorb Divine Love and Knowledge. This flurry of purple and silver light makes its way back to you. Once these light particles find you, breathe them in through your 9th, 8th, crown, third eye and throat chakras. Imagine your body filling up with purple and silver light. Breathe in 100% then exhale and release 20%.

Now it is time to thank the Universe for your clairvoyance, clairaudience, and clairsentience. Thank the Divine for all the other blessings in your life experienced and not yet experienced. Choose your words wisely and keep them grateful. (Gratitude is like a magnet, the more you thank the more you receive.) Set your intentions at this time. For example, your intention can be something like: "I invite the loving and healing energy that will support my querent and myself during and after this reading."

I like to close with "I am the sum total of Mother God, Father God, and my Souls Perfection", as I believe those are the energies now within me.

# Anchoring:

Anchoring is way to get your mind body and soul in a quick state of awareness. My anchoring statement is: I see, I hear, I feel, I know, I trust. I suggest you create a statement that resonates with you. If you have started your day with your meditation and get a call in the middle of the day to do a reading, you want to quickly reground, separate yourself energetically, redistribute your energy, and anchor.

Believe it or not, once you have this process down, it takes no more than 15 minutes, and can take as little as 5! It is a great way to start your day or any intuitive work. Just remember, when you are done with the intuitive work, reground yourself, turn your analyzer back on, and redistribute your energy so you have full use of all your energy centers. Just herd the energy of first four chakras energies (via color) back onto the elevator and go down to each "floor" one by one, until the elevator is empty. You may also want to adjust the wattage again so they are all shining at the same level.

Now you are ready to do some work!

# Intuitive vs. Formulative Readings

Many people start their tarot journey with a purchase of one or many of the tarot books available today. From there, they spend many hours studying card keys, memorizing meanings, and trying to gain an understanding of the Celtic Cross.

Often, they start the "Card-A-Day" practice, and feverishly journal their findings, until they become so bored with the practice, they stop. Then, a new deck or book gets their attention and they start all over again. My advice on this method of study:

# STOP

Stop memorizing and spend time with your cards. This is where we will start **courting your cards.** In the days of my parents youth, "courting" was what they did when they wanted to get to know someone they were interested in romantically. We can leave the romance portion of this metaphor out, but the idea is for you to get to know your tarot deck. The only tools required are a writing implement, any tarot deck you choose and an open mind.

You may have noticed when you purchased your tarot deck that it comes with either the "little white book" or a more substantial creator's version that often comes as part of a deluxe set. You may be asking yourself, "What the heck do I need a workbook for if all the answers are right here?" Let me respond to that thought, whether it is real (on your end) or imagined (on mine).

First, let me say that <u>I recommend you read either or both of those books</u> to get the writers perspective, ***after*** you have reviewed and experienced the deck yourself. You may find that, while some information resonates with you, some does not. I also want to point out the obvious: More often than not, the book author and deck creator (artist) are two different people working on the same project. Question: Have you ever worked on a project with someone...let's say a co-worker, partner, or spouse? Did you always agree? Probably not, and that is my point. That is why I recommend that you start by *first* getting to know the deck that inspired you to buy her (I will refer to tarot deck as "her" throughout the workbook), and then move toward the author's version. Equating decks to people, I know many people who I consider friends, who at times will volunteer information about someone I am about to meet in an effort to sway my opinion either positively or negatively. That is kind of what is happening when you read the authors book first, and why I recommend that you first get to know each card in your deck yourself, and *then* read what the author has to say.

# EleMental

For those of you new to tarot, each deck has four suits representing four different elements. The suits represent Fire, Water, Air, and Earth. According to various schools of philosophy, each element has a symbol, as seen below. It is important to note that each element also represents each human state: Physical, Mental, Spiritual and Emotional. It is important to recognize what the element means to you because, when doing readings, if there is a predominance of one suit, then you know that that specific energy is fueling the reading.

## Exercise 1:1

The following shapes below include symbols that represent each element. Review them for a moment. To really connect with the element, color in (or paste the color) that represents the symbol in the symbol itself. While doing this think about your conscious response to each element, and write it down. For example, you may say that fire makes you think of warmth, passion, high-energy, etc.

An equilateral red triangle is the symbol for fire.

What words come to mind when you think of fire? Write them here:

*Passion*

*energy*

*hot*

*light*

A solid silver crescent, with horns facing up is the symbol for water.

What words come to mind when you think of water? Write them here:

*Soothing   healing*
*relaxed   Emotion*
*Calm*

Air is represented by a solid blue circle.
What words come to mind when you think of air? Write them here:

*Carefree*

*Light*

*breezy*

Earth is a yellow solid square.
What words come to mind when you think of earth? Write them here:

*Strength*

*power*

Now that you have documented your conscious thoughts about the four elements, let's peer into your subconscious and see what else pops up.

# Exercise 1:2

The next exercise will take place over the next four days. *You will be able to start the additional exercises over the next four days too.* Each night, review an element and before you go to sleep tell yourself that the truth about that element will be revealed in your dreams. When you awake the next day, recall your dreams and document what you dreamt. See what is similar and what else popped up that you might not have consciously thought of.

For example, when I did this exercise for fire, I dreamt of someone I knew doing karate. In my dream, he was extremely physically fit. He and his opponent were playfully fighting – sparring really...not to cause harm but for training purposes. From this I related "**high energy**" (which matched my conscious thought) and added, "**sports**" to it, and could probably add "**exercise**" or "**training**". The same night, I had another dream about my mother and my aunt. In it, the dialog between us was funny, so I had to add "**humor**" to the list. My last dream of the night, (yes – I do tend to have a variety of vivid dreams!) involved me visiting a friend in an apartment I felt like I was in before. The interior design featured ergonomic wood shapes, green plants, and blank white spaces too. From this I determined **"creativity"** **"nature"**, and **"intuition"** could be added to my list.

[If you are one of those people who don't recall their dreams, meditate for a while before reviewing each symbol and see what images or words pop into your head.]

# Fire

<u>Conscious</u>                                          <u>Subconscious</u>

1.

2.

3.

4.

5.

6.

7.

8.

9.

10.

# Water

<u>Conscious</u>                                          <u>Subconscious</u>

1.

2.

3.

4.

5.

6.

7.

8.

9.

10.

# Air

<u>Conscious</u>                                         <u>Subconscious</u>

1.

2.

3.

4.

5.

6.

7.

8.

9.

10.

# Earth

<u>Conscious</u>                                         <u>Subconscious</u>

1.

2.

3.

4.

5.

6.

7.

8.

9.

10.

# Exercise 1:3

The next exercise involves you laying out each of the four suits of your deck in sequence (Ace through ten). Every deck has "given" elemental symbolisms; however, the purpose of this exercise is to take the lists you have created and match them up with the four suits of your deck. For example, based on your previous exercise, what do you feel is the "fire suit" in the deck you are studying now? What words or images came up (consciously and subconsciously) that matched your selected "fire" suit?

My Fire suit is _Swords_____ because:
- fire imagery        - Passionate images
- Powerful images

My Water suit is _Cups_____ because:
- water imagery    -communal healing (2, 3, 6, +9)
- Powerful emotions (love, happiness, sadness)

My Air suit is _Coins_____because:
- nomadic peoples (2, 5,)
- birds/reaching for the skies (ace, 4, 7, 8)

My Earth suit is _Wands_____because:
- Strong people
- warriors
- wands are an extension of power

# Emotion

In Mary K. Greer's book, *21 Ways to Read a Tarot Card*, the author suggests that tarot decks are metaphors of emotion (pgs. 18 -20), and I agree. If you haven't noticed it yet, you have an emotional reaction to each card in the deck. Pay attention. If you consider your emotion carefully, it can reveal where your psychic energy is being processed, and offers a strong indication of your "psychic type".

It has been said that there are five basic feeling constellations, which include joy, anger, sadness, fear, and disgust. Feelings of joy prompt you to keep doing what you are doing, while fear motivates you to move away. Anger tells you that your space has been violated and disgust is a survival mechanism – telling you that something is not good for you. Sadness is the most interesting as it causes us to review our grief and find the love behind it…it appears the more grief or sadness is felt, the stronger the love we have. Be sure to note if any of these feelings are included in your tarot card reviews.

## Exercise 2:1 Emotion

Start by going through your cards one by one and making a few "emotional reaction" piles. Spend at least a minute with each card really *breathing it in.*

Which cards made you happy? Pile number one! Which cards where you afraid of, visually? Pile number two. Which cards made you feel angry? Pile number three. Which cards gave you a feeling of disgust? Pile number four. There are pages for each of those stated emotions and a few blank pages so you can dedicate any other emotions that popped up as you reviewed your cards. *Note: The excessive space provided may be used in the future when you have added emotion cards, or have changed your mind down the road. Date your entries and use different colored pens if possible to see how you're your relationship with your deck evolves.

# Cards of Happiness/Joy

# Cards of Fear

# Cards of Sadness

# Cards of Anger

# Cards of _____

**Cards of** _____

# Cards of _____

# Exercise 2:2

You now have several "emotion piles". Start with one emotion pile and lay all the cards out. Spend some time reviewing each card as it is lying next to its neighboring emotion cards.

What, if anything, do the cards have in common? Are there the same colors, symbols, or animals on them? Which way are the people facing? How many people are on them? Write it down.

What are the differences with the cards in this chosen pile? Document it.

Take the time to review at least five of your emotion piles and document the similarities and differences below.

# Create a Story

## Exercise 3:1

ow, this is the fun part! Create a story using these cards. Story telling is an exercise that helps you to tap into another resource – your imagination, which is highly intuitive. In my workshops, I tell my classes that imagination and intuition are identical twins!

I wrote and self-published a novel entitled *"Dirty Laundry"*. It is a fun Chick-Lit novel, filled with sex, scandal, drama and, of course, tarot. People I knew inspired the characters but the story line was quite original and drawn completely from my imagination. As I completed the manuscript, a few events that I "invented" concerning particular characters in the story actually happened. One of the two main characters was the victim of adultery. In the story line, it was splashed all over the gossip tabloids and resulted in divorce. A childhood friend of mine, who was one of two people who served as my inspiration for this character, had that exact series of events happen to her. In the story, I even described the "other woman" and sure enough, the "other woman" in real-life looked exactly as described!

Yet another character was inspired by a dear, pleasantly plump friend of mine. Knowing what a weight conscious society we are, for the sake of the story, I described the character a good 75 lbs. thinner. Fast forward, my friend lost 75lbs. on Weight Watchers.

Lastly, the other main character (who if you read the book and met me, you know that _she is_ me) had a challenging relationship with her husband and by the end of the book, considers a complete lifestyle change, which included a divorce. Well, if you haven't figured it out yet, not only did my husband and I divorce, but I am happily living with my…Ahem….*female* partner whom I met after about 3 years *after* publishing the book.

**Directions**: Lay the cards down in rows next to each other so that it tells a story of your making. Write it down. *<u>Note</u>: This exercise stimulates your imagination and also helps you thread together your personal interpretation of your deck.

Suggested Exercise:

Do this with each emotion you have noted. There are a few blank pages for your Emotion Stories.

## Suggested Reading

*21 Ways to Read a Tarot Card,* by Mary K. Greer: The emotion chapter (pages 15 – 23 & 243 – 244)

**My _____ Story:**

**My _____Story**

# My _____Story

# Recreate a Story

## Exercise 4:1

This is another exercise that helps you learn to thread the story in your cards. Think of a book you have read or movie you watched and create a spread telling that story. For example, I watched a suspenseful horror movie called *The Last House on The Left* and came up with the following spread, using my Morgan Greer deck:

Card 1: 10 of Swords (Death)
Card 2: Judgment Reversed (A family trying to move past pain of the past)
Card 3: The Fool (Vacation, New beginnings)
Card 4: Knight of Swords Reversed (Bully)
Card 5: 5 of Swords (Stab in the back)
Card 6: 3 of Swords (Pain, Heartache tears)
Card 7: King of Swords Reversed (Revenge)
Card 8: 6 of Swords (Escape)

What is your movie/book? Create your story using as many cards as needed.

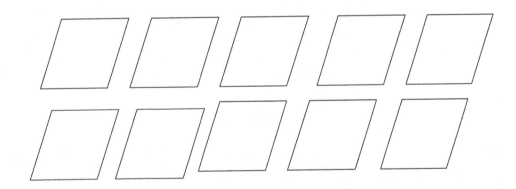

# Suit Stories

## Exercise 5:1

This exercise requires a little room, and a lot of imagination. As a reminder, imagination and intuition are identical twins - so give yourself permission to have fun.

Lay out all of your numbered cards (Ace through ten) in a horizontal row, via suit. Start with the suit of Wands, (Ace through ten) and then segue to the Pentacles, Swords, and finally Cups. **Part I** of this exercise is to review the story by suit with your deck.

**Example:** For this exercise, I am using my Morgan Greer deck.

My Wands story is not very complicated…it starts: "Once upon a time there was an amazing idea floating around in the sky, waiting for someone to find it and make it real (Ace of Wands). Two people discovered the idea at the same time (2 of Wands), but only one had the vision and organizational skills to bring it to light (3 of Wands). I will call him Luke.  Luke took the plan and created a strong foundation for it (4 of Wands) and as soon as he did so, everyone wanted to get in the act, and there was fighting about how to execute it (5 of Wands). Luke decided that, since none of these "coat tail rider's" had a clue or knew how to do anything with this idea, he would choose how to execute the vision (6 of Wands). He stood his ground (7 of Wands) and quickly received word (8 of Wands) that the King himself wanted Luke *and Luke only* to move forward with his idea, banning anyone to interfere (9 of Wands). Finally, without anyone's help or assistance, Luke was left to carry this idea out on his own, and felt burdened in the process (10 of Wands).

That is my version of The Suit of Wands *today,* and I give myself permission to change it when I feel the need.

Create a story for each of your suits.

# My Wand Story

# My Pentacle Story

# My Sword Story

# My Cup Story

# I've Got Your Number

**Part 2:** Again, this exercise requires that you place each suit of your cards in row, horizontally. This time we are going to take a look at the numbered cards for stories. Start with the Aces. When you look at all four Aces, how do you feel? If it makes it easier, place them left to right (since that is the way we are used to reading).

When I look at my Aces (still using Morgan Greer), the short story I see is: Once upon a time, there was a great idea floating (Ace of Wands) that could yield a lot of money (Ace of Pentacles). It may be a fight, (Ace of Swords) but could make me really happy (Ace of Cups). To sum it up, I feel like the cards are full of potential, but not a real promise. While the potential feels good to me, I know that there is a lot of work to make this potential become reality. So now, when I see four Aces in a reading, I say to my client, there is a lot of potential in the air that requires a lot of work. Does that make sense?

Now - let's take an Ace away. What happens now? I now remove the Ace of Cups and feel like the remaining three Aces speak to me of important news (with the Wands and Swords) and it still "feels" good. If I remove another Ace (Swords), I see an opportunity for a new creative endeavor or job where one could earn a lot of money. If I combine the Ace of Pentacles and Ace of Cups, I am on cloud nine!

Take the time to do this exercise so you can see how multiples work for you in your deck. The interesting thing about this exercise is that each deck may yield different impressions. My Morgan Greer deck has only one person featured on the "2's" of each suit with the exception of the Cups. My Mythic Tarot Deck has two people featured on the 2 of Cups, three people featured on the 2 of Swords, only one person (and a centaur) featured on the Wands and one person on the 2 of Pentacles. Those who come to tarot via Numerology will have strong feelings associated with the numbers themselves, but when you come to tarot intuitively it may yield different results depending on your deck.

Note: Numerology is an amazing study. Many avoid it due to the "math"; however, if you feel drawn down that path, I encourage pursuing it.

## My Multiple Meanings

# Personal Numerology

Speaking of numerology, let us take a moment to introduce ourselves to what I will call "Personal Numerology". There may be similarities or differences between this and real numerology, but we are doing this to get in touch with our intuition...not win a Numerology prize. This exercise is helpful when you have to determine what is going on with a client. I often take the numbered cards add them up, reduce them to a single digit, and then throw in my personal numerology interpretation. This is really easy. First, think of something that you love to do that is creative. Do you like to write, cook, or draw? For the sake of this exercise, we will use cooking. So we have just decided that we are going to bake cookies....yum! Let's call the initial thought "ace" and the finished cookies "ten".

Now ask yourself: What happens in between?

- Ace: Hmmm...I think I am going to make cookies! *(Idea)*
- Two: Decide what kind of cookies *(Planning)*
- Three: Get the ingredients..*(Work)*
- Four: Make the batter...*(Create foundation)*
- Five: Take a taste. Do you need to make any changes...? *(Keep going, start over or change plan)*
- Six: Grab the cookie cutter...*(Choice made)*
- Seven: Place it in the pan and pop it in the oven.... *(Reflect on work and look forward to outcome)*
- Eight: I smell success! *(Seeing the beginnings of completion.)*
- Nine: The cookies are done...just cooling now! *(Knowing the fruits yielded from your labor.)*
- Ten: Fresh cookies on a plate! *(Completion!)*

Try this example with something you really love to do, and literally go through this exercise yourself to see what each number means for you.

**I love to** _____**and this is my process:**

**Ace:**

**Two:**

**Three:**

**Four:**

**Five:**

**Six:**

**Seven:**

**Eight:**

**Nine:**

**Ten:**

**Special Note:** When you match your creative process with a suit, what suit do you come up with? Go back and now review your elements and suit stories. Note the similarities and differences. Note what now really resonates within you.

# Common-Sensing Your Deck

This workbook is about developing your intuition, and I believe that our senses are connected to our Chakras, which, as we have seen, help us determine intuitive types. This portion of *The Intuitive Tarot Workbook* is dedicated to our five senses: Feeling, Hearing, Smelling, Tasting, and Seeing.

The next series of exercises is designed for you to incorporate your five senses when taking in your cards.

## Exercise 6:1 Feeling

Select any card from your deck. For this exercise, I have selected *The Fool* from my Buckland Romani Tarot deck.

Look at your card very closely for at least 30 seconds. Breathe in through your nose. Hold it for five to ten seconds and exhale out through your mouth. Repeat the breathing exercise three times, or until you feel relaxed. Now, what do you feel? (When I look at my card, I feel a slight wind in my face.) Trust that feeling and document it.

Go through your deck and continue to select cards that produce an effect you can feel. Write down the cards and those specific feelings you sense.

I once had a querent who had a 10 of Swords in her spread. Upon seeing it, I felt a quick sharp pain in my back. I asked if she had "back issues". She replied that she did. I then asked if she had tried acupuncture – which she had just recently started and it was working for her. Note: I had found both my acupuncture and back pain card! Trust what you sense and you will be rewarded!

**Note**: When doing readings for others, you may experience physical pains related to *them*. (This identifies you as a Physical Intuitive.) This is especially true when the cards in front of you have a similar or partnering image (like the pain I felt when I saw the ten of Swords). When you have this experience, it is especially important to go through the preliminary exercises upon completion of the reading.

# Cards I Can Feel:

Dedicate the next couple of pages to documenting the feelings you get from certain cards in your deck. You may have cards where you feel nothing. That may change over time. The most important aspect of these exercises is that you are opening up your intuitive senses with an attitude of expectation. Revisit this exercise in 30 days to see what cards you can add to your list.

Also, keep in mind that when you are reading others, you may experience or feel something physically that you never felt before. Or you may suddenly get a headache or a ringing in your ears, and think it is you. Once you are in "Intuitive Space" realize that everything matters and that what you feel is probably from an outside source, your client. You are identifying with them. Remember, when we are reading others, we are opening up to them intuitively accessing "tachyons" not "quarks". When our client speaks to us and we hear them, we are accepting information via the quark system. However, when our client sits in front of us and we access information about the past, present or future, or experience a physical pain we never had before, (and when they leave, the pain also leaves), we are accessing information via tachyons.

*This is important to remember because there are cards that may mean one thing to you when you are reading yourself, but something entirely different when combined with someone else's energy.*

# Cards I Can Feel

# Exercise 6:2 Hearing

Still using my Buckland Romani deck, I pulled *The World* card for the next exercise.

Pull a card from your deck. Look at your card very closely for at least 30 seconds. Breathe in through your nose, hold it for 10 seconds and exhale out through your mouth. Do this three times. What do hear? (When I look at my card, I hear the bells on the woman's skirt.) Trust what you hear and document it.

Note: You may go through your deck only "hearing" a few cards – that is fine. As your relationship develops with your cards, that may change. And remember, TRUST YOURSELF. I was surprised one day to hear the lyrics to a song by SCRIPT, while I was doing a reading. The song just popped into my head – not particularly referring to any one card, but the story the cards were telling. I could have blown it off, and decided to I trust it. I recited them to my querent (No, I did not sing to her!). She was shocked and tearfully told me that she wrote those same lyrics to her boyfriend.

Again, you may not hear anything the first time you do this exercise, but keep yourself open to the experience. The next two pages are dedicated to the cards you can hear.

# Cards I Can Hear

# Cards I Can Hear

# Exercise 6:3 Smelling

No, you haven't reached the scratch and sniff portion of the book! You are now going to select a card. (I have selected Tower from my Morgan Greer deck.)

Look at your card very closely for at least 30 seconds. Breathe in through your nose. Hold it for five to ten seconds and exhale out through your mouth. Repeat this three times. Since we are "intuitively-smelling" this card, take another deep breath through your nose, hold it for ten seconds and exhale again. What do you smell? (When I breathe in my card, I smell smoke.) Trust the smell and document it.

Go through your deck and continue to select cards that produce an olfactory effect. Write down the cards and the specific smells. If there is a card that you can "Smell and Feel", document that too.

<u>Side Note</u>: I once had a querent who was having issues with her teenage son. When I pulled The Tower for her reading, I had an overwhelming 'smelling sensation' of smoke. When I said this to her, she revealed that she had recently discovered her son was experimenting with marijuana.

On yet another day, I was driving with my daughter and suddenly smelled the fragrance of a very close friend of mine, whom I hadn't seen in years and who lives in another state. I asked my daughter if she was wearing perfume, and she wasn't. When another wave of fragrance hit me, I pulled over to the side of the road and called my friend. She answered her cell phone and informed me that she was sitting outside the hospital - where her mother was in intensive care. She said, "I was just thinking of you."

You will find that when you trust your five senses in intuitive work, your sixth sense will kick in, creating an "overlap" in your mundane activities with your psychic senses. All that is required is trust in **you**.

# Cards I Can Smell

# Cards I Can Smell

# Exercise 6:4 Tastes

To be perfectly honest with you, until writing this book, I never "tasted" a card before. So for this exercise, I went through my Hanson Roberts deck in search of a card I could find with a gustatory effect. I was immediately drawn to the 6 of pentacles. This card (with this deck) features an older gregarious looking man holding a scale in his right hand and offering a pentacle from his left. The scale is balanced and each side contains a pentacle. There are two children looking up at him with wide-eyed (and mouth) wonder. One child holds a bag waiting to receive this wonderful pentacle gift from the older man. With this card, I *smell and taste* sugar cookies. The next couple of pages are dedicated to taste!

Center yourself with the breathing exercise, and review your deck to find cards you can "taste". Taste and smell are closely related – so allow yourself to open up to this. If you were able to smell a card, you will be able to taste one too.

# Cards I Can Taste

# Seeing is Believing

## Exercise 6:5

Now we will take the visual aspect of connecting with your cards *beyond emotion*. This is a version of personal symbolism – which we will do more with later.

Select any card from your deck and look at it closely. (I have selected the 6 of Pentacles again, this time from my Morgan Greer deck.) While looking at your card, breathe deeply through your nose. Hold it for 10 seconds and exhale through your mouth. Repeat three times.

My card depicts a man generously offering money to unknown adult recipients (you can only see their adult size hands) with one hand, while holding an empty, balanced scale in the other. That describes the picture, but when I look at it, *for me*, it is a doctor giving someone a pill. When I pull this card, I have asked my querents if they are on medication (the surrounding cards are also helpful) and I am usually right – even though this is not the traditional meaning of the card. When you trust yourself, you are rewarded!

<u>**IMPORTANT NOTE**</u>: Notice that I drew the 6 of Pentacles from my Hanson Roberts deck. With that version of the card, I smelled and tasted sugar cookies. There were no sugar cookie thoughts, smells, or tastes remotely connected to the 6 of Pentacles in my Morgan Greer deck.

**Worth Mentioning**: My interpretation does not have to be the same as yours even if the cards we select are the same. I think of reading tarot the way I think of dream interpretation. While I have several dream interpretation books, I believe that dreams are subjective and cannot be interpreted the same way for everyone.

For example, a dream interpretation book may define a dream of kittens as a "pet project". Well, I am severely allergic to cats (not kittens), so if I dream of kittens it represents something that can turn into a life threatening situation because kittens grow up into cats.

**One final note on this subject**: You may find as you work with the cards that something in the card catches your eye. Say aloud what "it" is, to get clarity. I have had numerous readings where an image holds my attention and when I mention the image itself, I get validation. Example: While reading a querent on a relationship issue, the image of the crossed keys on The Hierophant held my attention. I asked, "What is going on with keys?" She confessed that her boyfriend asked for his keys back.

You may experience only one or two of these sensations when you start this practice. That is fine. Again, you are now opening yourself up to the possibility of having these experiences, so they will now start to flow in.

The blank pages following are dedicated to what your cards mean to you as you work with them.

# Personal Meanings

# Personal Meanings

# Personal Meanings

# Personal Meanings

# Metaphorically Speaking

A metaphor, as defined by Webster's dictionary is: "A figure of speech in which a term is transferred from the object it ordinarily designates to an object it may designate only by complicit comparison or analogy". (And that is why I hate Webster's Dictionary...what did I just say??? Speak English, Webster!!!)

To clarify (in my words) – a metaphor refers to a saying that likens one thing to something else in an effort to get your point across. For example, saying, "I am dog tired" refers to the fact that you are tired enough to want to sleep (because dogs sleep a lot). Or, my personal favorite, "He is knee high to a grass hopper..." – meaning: "The man is short".

There are quite a few cards that will make you think of metaphors. When I look at the Ace of Cups in my Morgan Greer deck I feel like "My cup runneth over" or when I look at the 10 of Swords in the Morgan Greer, it is the "stab in the back" card. (Not true in my Buckland Romany deck – where the victim is stabbed in the front.)

Go through your deck in search of metaphors and write them down.

# Exercise 7: My Metaphors

# Exercise 8: Naming Names

What I love about this exercise is that I stumbled across it by accident and validated it in practice.

I love my Buckland Romani deck. I find it amazing for a variety of reasons. Originally, I was attracted to the vivid colors on the deck - I have found that color sparks my intuition. More importantly, I love that there is an ethnic variety in the entire deck that is more representative of reality then so many traditional decks (at least _my_ reality!) The people depicted in the cards vary in appearance so much that their personality seems to ooze right off the card. For example, when I look at the Page of Chives (Page of Swords) I am looking at Brad Pitt, The Knight of Koros (Cups) is Kevin Bacon, Penelope Cruz is The Star, and Gena Davis is the Queen of Koshes (Wands).

During a reading when I identify a person in any of the cards, I start by mentioning the name (Brad) and then go into other "B" male names (Brandon, Brian, etc.) and end up touching on the name of someone the querent knows. The identities are not limited to famous people: The King of Wands in my Hanson Roberts deck looks just like James, my close friend - who's nick name is Goldie. In this case I use both hard G's and soft G's to "name" the person. Many cards in the Buckland Romani deck seem to remind me of people I know - in fact the High Priestess looks like my mother.

**Note:** I, like many of you, have been studying many subjects these days in an effort to put "more tools in my toolbox" so to speak. Healing has been an important subject for me, and I have studied a variety of energy healing modalities including Colin Tipping's Chakra Clearing, Traditional Reiki, Donna Eden's Energy Healing, and Dr. Eric Pearl's Reconnective Healing. During the latter, it was mentioned in the workshop that Reconnective Healing accesses new frequencies that allows us to be a conduit of love, light, and information. It is a very simple process that works extremely well.

I transfer this information and apply it to learning tarot. I believe that these "new frequencies" make themselves available (in part) through technology and that traditional decks, while valid and important, do not offer as much information as the decks that access the newer technology. Montage style decks (Voyager, Gendron, Vision Tarot, and Cosmic Tribe to name a few) are excellent for picking up specific information you may not glean from the Rider-Waite deck. In my workshops many of my students also find this to be true. This is my personal opinion and you are certainly welcome to discover for yourself the validity of that observation.

Now - go through your deck and see if there are any familiar faces. Take the next page and write down which cards remind you of someone. When you try this technique in a reading, document which card/name identifications work.

<u>Note</u>: When you meet new people, ask yourself who they remind you of in your deck. Also, jot down why.

## Who is who?

1.  My _____reminds me of:
2.  My _____reminds me of:
3.  My _____reminds me of:
4.  My _____reminds me of:
5.  My _____reminds me of:
6.  My _____reminds me of:
7.  My _____reminds me of:
8.  My _____reminds me of:
9.  My _____reminds me of:
10. My _____reminds me of:
11. My _____reminds me of:
12. My _____reminds me of:
13. My _____reminds me of:
14. My _____reminds me of:
15. My _____reminds me of:
16. My _____reminds me of:
17. My _____reminds me of:
18. My _____reminds me of:

# Personal Symbolism

*"Symbols are visible representations of an invisible intangible reality-something from inside is revealed in the world outside, something spiritual in something concrete, something special in something ordinary."*

— *Verena* Cast's forward in *"Tarot and Individuation"*

## Exercise 9:

The more you experience life, the better you will be able to read tarot. One of the methodologies used in tarot is symbolism. There are several books that you can refer to regarding traditional interpretations. I have listed a few in the bibliography. What we are going to ponder here are *personal symbols*.

This exercise will take a bit more of your of effort. Ten times throughout your day, connect whatever you are doing, observing or hearing, to your tarot deck. Simply ask yourself, "Which card does this activity remind me of?" or, "What does this advertisement have to do with my *blank* tarot deck?" or "This song reminds me of which card?" For example, the task of writing this book reminds me of my eight of pentacles in my Druid deck.

**Personal Note:** When we do a reading, we are drawing from *what we know to be true based on our experience*. Therefore, there can be a "filter" over your "intuitive view finder".

Many people who see you for a reading may think every word that comes out of your mouth is a "premonition". I often start off with pleasantries to get my clients relaxed – before I actually "turn on" – but my clients don't always get that. They may start asking questions that I (as Gina) answer. Therefore, I make it a regular practice to say, "This is me speaking, not the cards." So they know the difference.

Note: You won't always attract clients who resonate with your references. I will never forget the client early on in my career that, while reading his cards, I offered that his reading indicated: "There is something you want to stop doing but it feels like you can't."

His reply was "That must be the masturbation and pornography." I thought he was joking and I didn't only laugh...I guffawed loudly! Guess what? *He wasn't joking.* My reference, regarding his comment, was one of humor because it sounded like something my sister would say in jest...(oh well!)

**Tip:** Be ever mindful of your references.

# Exercise 10:

The following exercise involves you recognizing what in your life reminds you of what card.

Document your activity, image, or song with the card in the following space provided.

# Energy In Motion (or E >Motion)

*"The best tarot readers are usually gifted empaths who use their emotional genius, consciously or unconsciously as a major component of their intuitive and communicative skills."*

– Mary K. Greer, *21 Ways to Read a Tarot Card*

Being familiar with your energy centers and how each respond to stimuli is paramount as an intuitive reader. As Mary Greer states, many of the best tarot readers are gifted empaths. Empaths pick up and respond to the energy of others.

I was invited to give an Intuitive Tarot Workshop to a group of people just starting their journey with tarot. We practiced an exercise I learned from the *Guide to the Sacred Rose Tarot* by Johanna Gargiulo-Sherman, and modified so my students didn't feel the "pressure" of doing a reading.

The room was filled with many tarot novices – in fact, many did not even own tarot decks. However, by the end of the class, several had demonstrated a very keen intuitive sense that became obvious with this one simple exercise, which is now one of my favorites when teaching.

We started by separating the Major Arcana from my Buckland Romani deck, shuffling the cards. I requested a volunteer to select a single card. (I selected this deck because there were no distracting words on the Major Arcana cards, just vivid pictures and a discreet number on the bottom of the card.) I fanned the cards in front of my student placed them face down and he chose The Emperor.

The card features a bearded man sitting cross-legged in a simple wooden chair. He is well dressed, and holds a scepter in his left hand and balances a teacup in his lap. There is a knife stuck in the floor by his chair. His shoes are polished and he wears black slacks, a blue blazer, a sweater vest, shirt, and tie. He sports a big ring on the middle finger of his right hand. The room he sits in is a warm golden yellow color. On the sides and bottom of the walls are painted plants; and over his head, where he sits, is something that looks like a wheel.

The exercise calls for each student to hold the card under another student's chin, breathe in the card, looking into the querents eyes, review the energy over his/her

81

head, and tell a story beginning with "Once upon a time". There were no expectations on anyone to "foretell" upcoming events.

However, what happened was amazing. Although we used the same card for everyone, each student, with the exception of one, gave an accurate description of an important person in their querent's life. Laura, the student who read me gave an amazing character description of my ex-husband (unbeknownst to her) and how he maintained a position of importance in my life – which is true. <u>Note</u>: Laura was new to tarot; she was one of 4 students that did not own a deck! The only person who did not give an accurate description was a student so overwhelmed by her "reading" that she was at a loss for words and did not give a reading at all.

<u>Important to note</u>: Here is an example of the interpretation of one card having a variety of "truths" and that energy combines with the image to provide information.

# Exercise 11 – Aura Readings

Try this exercise with a minimum of three volunteers, using the same card. Start by selecting a major Arcana card and placing it under the chin of your subject - picture side facing you. Look into the eyes of your subject for a moment. Breathe him or her in. Then, without moving your head, look about 8 inches above their head, where the eighth chakra would be. (Don't worry about whether or not you see colors – auras can be perceived.) Look at the card again. State what you feel the card means to your volunteer. You can use "Once upon a time" to start your statement.

How did your subject react? Document your findings below.

# Time to Meet the Majors

This is an exercise I learned from (the brilliant) Marcus Katz in his book, *Tarosophy* (who gives credit to Edwin C. Steinbrecher).

This exercise is called, *The Inner Guide Meditation*. It will not only allow you to eventually meet all of the Major Arcana cards in your deck, but will also allow you to meet your Spirit Guide. This meditation requires a minimum of 20 minutes of quiet time.

It follows a number of recognized steps in a specific sequence – in fact, it is mentioned in Steinbrecher's book, that only by following these specific steps can you meet your <u>true</u> spirit guide.

<u>Note</u>: This mediation must be done from your own personal view – *<u>not as if you are watching a movie.</u>*

Start by taking a few deep breaths through your nose, hold for five seconds and exhale through the mouth. Before starting this meditation – be sure to ground, center, redistribute your energy, and set your intentions. It is very important that you turn off your "analyzer" so that you are a receiver.

1. Visualize a beach with your back to the sea.
2. See a cave off in the distance.
3. Walk to the cave and enter it.
4. Once you have identified the smells, feelings, and sounds associated with this cave, walk to the back of the cave and find an opening or doorway **to your left.**
5. Walk out into this new landscape...how does it differ?
6. Call for your animal totem/guide to take you to where you may meet your Spirit Guide, which will be **off to the right.**
7. Once the animal joins you, follow him/her to your Guide.
8. Follow the animal until you get to the feet of your Guide.
9. Test your Guide by asking that they take your right hand in his left (reversed if you are left handed) and transmit their feelings toward you. (You should experience an intense amount of love. If you do not experience this, ask the animal to take you to your true Guide.)
10. Ask your inner guide to show you a representation of one of the Major Arcana cards. You may start with the Sun, Moon, Star, or Wheel of Fortune and move to

"people", if that is comfortable for you. You can even ask that the Sun/Moon/ Star/Wheel take human form – so you can communicate with it. When I did this exercise and went to The Wheel Of Fortune, he appeared as a very large Egyptian man, who spoke with his arms crossed throughout our visit. Be sure to give the image permission to penetrate any blocks that may be up send all the love and light into you as you can physically take. ***You should feel something palpable.***

11. Ask the card you selected to tell you how you can honor its energies in your daily life and what gift it has for you. (Guides NEVER say anything negative and are not loquacious by nature.)

When you feel you feel you have completed this initial task in its entirety, confirm with your Guide. Allow the totem to take you back to the cave and exit to the beach.

~

Another popular practice taught by many tarot scholars, has you "step into a card". This is another great way to develop a personal relationship with each of your cards, and takes a minimum of 22 days.

For that simpler exercise – all you are really doing is the following:

- Go through your preliminary exercises.
- Select a card from your major Arcana.
- Breathe in the card with three deep breaths or more, capturing the image on the card.
- Close your eyes and try to recall every detail of the card in your mind's eye.
- "Blow up" the card to the size of a window directly in front of you. If your deck has a border, it can act as a windowpane.
- Step through the window and into the card.
- Breathe in the new space…do you smell, hear, see anything unusal?
- Meet the character in the card. Introduce yourself. Ask it questions (i.e., What should I know about you? How do you manifest in my life? What is my personal meaning of you?)
- When ready thank them and say goodbye.
- Step into yourself.
- Reground.

**The next 22 pages are dedicated to "Meeting your Major's".**

# Fool Major

# Magician Major

# High Priestess Major

# Empress Major

# Emperor Major

# Hierophant Major

# Lovers Major

# The Chariot Major

# Strength (or Justice) Major

# The Hermit Major

# The Wheel of Fortune Major

# Justice (or Strength) Major

# The Hanged Man Major

# Death Major

# Temperance Major

# The Devil Major

# The Tower Major

# The Star Major

# The Moon Major

# The Sun Major

# Judgment Major

# The World Major

# Spread 'Em!

S o, now that you are developing a relationship with your deck, note that, just like your relationships with your friends, it will continue to evolve. Are you ready for readings? Great! I offer suggestions here that will allow you to read for yourself and others immediately.

The Celtic Cross (which is neither a cross nor of Celtic origin) is the most popular spread in tarot use, and can be complicated to master. There are several books that offer insight into this subject, and even here, many disagree. Some authors will say to start this spread by picking a card out of the deck representing the client, and then shuffle and lay out the cross. I believe that removing a card from the deck prior to a reading is like playing a piano with one key missing or trying to write a book without the use of the letter "C". The tarot deck is a complete "book" and you can't get the gist of the "book" if a page is missing! (There are 2 ways around this: Either use a card from another deck, or agree on a card with your client and ***do not*** pull it from the deck. If it shows up in the reading, it will help offer insight based on its placement).

The purpose of this book is for you to further your relationship with your deck. Creating your own spreads is a way to continue your development. It is very easy to do, and you will be able to learn how your cards "react" with each other. Think of it as doing your favorite exercise with your new friend!

Shuffle your cards; think of a burning question you have about your life right now, and do something simple such as a 3-card spread. Document your question and reading below.

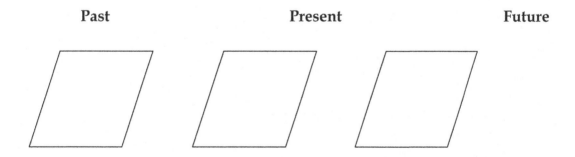

Past       Present       Future

**Card 1 Past:**
**Card 2 Present:**
**Card 3 Future:**

**What do you think this means today?**

**Looking back:** What do you think it means one week from now (put date here and see how it plays out!)

<u>Note</u>: An exercise I learned from Mary K. Greer includes moving the "time" cards around to gain perspective. By shifting the cards around, you can see how you may feel about the future when it is in your past or how you feel about your present when it is in your past...try it!

If you like the idea of a Significator, then select a card from another deck to be the Significator, and place that card in the beginning, or if you really want to get fancy, place it in the middle and do something like this:

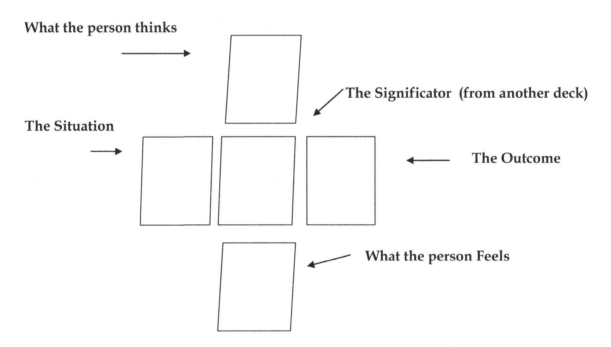

**What the person thinks**

**The Significator (from another deck)**

**The Situation**

**The Outcome**

**What the person Feels**

**Document your question here:**
**Document the card representing what the person thinks:**
**The Situation:**
**What the person Feels:**
**The Outcome:**
**Looking back at the Outcome:**

# Notes On Your Readings

# The Analysis of The Celtic Cross

Because the Celtic cross is the most popular spread known to tarot enthusiasts and querents, I would be remiss if I did not at least introduce you to it. There are many ways to "learn" the spread. I recommend you select one way and stick with it. For this reason I have not placed a number designating where the cards go on the following diagram. While on the subject of numbers, just because the cards are placed in sequence, it doesn't mean you have to read in sequence. It doesn't mean you start your reading with the first card and read to the tenth. Personally, I get the gist of the entire spread and start with where my eyes are drawn to in relation to the question.

1. **This is what covers you.** This card reveals what your client is experiencing in regard to the question. If a court card shows up here, it indicates that another person is involved.

2. **This is what crosses you for good or bad.** This card can be determined in the light of the remainder of the spread.

3. **This is the basis of the situation.** This card reveals the *origin* of your clients question. Sometimes the question (or the client) does not reveal the whole situation, so pay attention to the card here. For example, if the client were to ask "Will Joe contact me?" - you may find by looking at the card here, that there has been a fight, or just a separation due to travel. Either way, paying close attention to this card is helpful.

4. **This is behind you** – or in the process of leaving. You can tell from this card the immediate background vibrations experienced by the client. The client's attitude can impact a lot, so a negative card here indicates the client is still carrying some "baggage".

5. **This is what crowns you and could come into being.** This card offers a possible, often probable course of future events.

6. **This is before you.** This card, along with the tenth card, reveals the outcome. The sixth card *leads to* the tenth, and both deal with the future that is taking shape as a result of past and present circumstances.

7. **This represents your fear or apprehension.** This card and the third card reveal the true emotions surrounding the client's original question.

8. **This represents the feelings of those around you.** If the client asked a question about another person, this card will reveal the other person's point of view. If the client's question is regarding their personal activities (work/love life), this card will reveal how they are viewed by others.

9. **This represents your own positive feelings.** Often a person thinks one thing, but through fear may say something entirely different. This card will help you understand how he or she really feels about their situation.

10. **This is the outcome.** All of the other nine cards lead to this one, and must be read together to tell the "story".

**<u>Gina's Celtic Cross Poem</u>:** I created this years ago and found it helpful. Borrow this one or make up one that suits you!
Covers, Crosses, Basis, Behind…
Crowns, Before you, Negative mind…
Feelings of others…feelings you own…
This is the outcome…the future is known.

**Write Your Version Below:**

# Timing and Tarot

A great basic way to determine timing with tarot is through "Season Cards". I generally use earth based religions as my guide, however astrologers use a different method. Choose one and stick to it. With some decks, you may note that the artist/creator has chosen seasons for you, based on their beliefs.

## The four Aces represent the Seasons & Directions:

- Ace of Cups: Spring or March, April, May/West
- Ace of Wands: Summer or June, July, August/South
- Ace of Swords: Autumn or September, October, November/East
- Ace of Pentacles: Winter or December, January, February/North

## Astrologer's version:

- Ace of Cups: Summer/North
- Ace of Wands: Spring/East
- Ace of Swords: Fall/West
- Ace of Pentacles: Winter/South

~

## Relating the Season to the Celtic Cross

Timing can be determined from positions 5, 6, 7, 8, and 9. If the Ace is in any one of these five positions, it indicates the time of year involved. So, if the Ace of Cups falls in position 6, this indicates that the "event" will occur sometime in the Spring Season (March, April, or May).

## Determining the Week

Once you determined the season, you can then move to card 10 to determine the week. If there is a **numbered card** in position 10, that tells you what week in the season the event is likely to occur.

For example, if we have an Ace of Cups in position 5, 6, 7, 8, or 9, and card 10 is a 3 of Swords, the event will occur 3 weeks into the summer season (or about the second week in July).

If a court card appears at position 10, a person will be involved in the outcome, and the next (I should say "Previous") numbered card will help determine the week.

If a Major Arcana is at position 10, this indicates significant importance. (Due to the value of the Major Arcana/Higher cosmic forces will be active on that date and prove to be meaningful). If the card is a double digit card, reduce it to a single digit.

# All About Me Tarot

Let us now take a look at your past. People are often hesitant to look into the future. When looking into the past, there is nothing to be afraid of – you have already survived! While there never is anything to fear, this will help you get comfortable handling and interpreting your cards.

This process is an adaptation of a process taught in Mary K. Greer's "*Tarot for Yourself*". The difference is that you will be using your *personal intuitive insight* that you have developed in the process of getting acquainted with your deck.

Get a "big picture" view of your life by reflecting on five major turning points. They may represent choices you made in the past (like getting married) or those made for you (like getting a divorce). Some choices may be times in your life when you could have continued on the path you were on but chose not to (ie: such as a move out of your home state for a new "internet relationship"), as opposed to finding someone local and staying put. Recall those times when you agonized over a decision AND also the times when it seemed events were predestined. These milestones taught you the lessons that have led you to who you are and where you are today.

**Events:**

1.

2.

3.

4.

5.

Next, select the Court cards which can represent "inner" parts of you – so a Page can represent your inner child, a King can represent your more assertive side (if you're a woman) or a Queen can represent your nurturing side (if you're a man). Note these next to the "Events".

Next, select a Minor card representing the "Event". The 4 of Wands, for example, can represent getting married.

Next, select a Major Arcana card using meanings you discovered during your **Inner Guide Meditation** to represent why you made the choices you did. (One card can represent several events).

Now briefly sum up each event in a five-card spread. List your summary below:

**Events/Court card/ Minor Arcana/Major Arcana**

1.
2.
3.
4.
5.

Note by your selections:

Were you active or passive in your situations? What were the motivating factors behind your choices? Looking back on these choices, what do you wish you could "redo"?

Questions:

- Is there a dominant suit in each event?
- Based on your personal interpretations, what does that suggest to you?
- What outstanding significance do you note? (For example are there particular colors, number of people, or any symbolism that is redundant or speaks to you personally?)

Write anything you find significant in the space provided below.

# All About Me Notes

# Are You A Swinger?

Pendulums amplify information which is coming from your higher self. The easiest way to approach pendulum use is to simply ask yes/no questions. The first thing you need to identify is which movement indicates a "Yes" is and which movement indicates a "No". I have often read that you need to "ensure steadiness" when using a pendulum, but I have found in my healing work that even if you are moving around you will get accuracy. Hold your pendulum in your hand by the end of the chain or string. Take a few deep breaths. Next, simply ask a question to your pendulum such as "Is my name George?" Wait a moment to clarify the direction and get a steady movement. Next, ask, "Is my name (*insert your name here*)?" Viola! You now know your pendulums "yes "and "no" movements!

When you get information in your reading that is confusing to you, you can now just ask your pendulum for clarity. Be sure to keep track of your findings. <u>Note</u>: If you are 'wishy-washy', your pendulum will be as well.

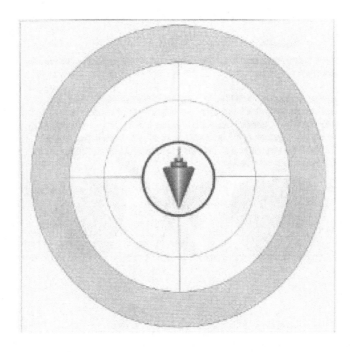

# Personal Tidbits

## Clairvoyant Tips

Once you really get to know your deck, the one thing I like to do before a client comes is run my "tools" (preliminary exercises) and then ask The Universe to show me a few cards to give me a clue. The cards ALWAYS come up in a reading.

I learned to practice this process one day when I forgot I had an appointment with a client. After my initial freak out, I figured out how I could meet her, (she was so patient and wonderful - and I was going to be *so* late!). I then realized I did not have my cards with me. After figuring out how I could deal with <u>that</u> (I called the location to see if they had a particular deck) I then had the calm and patience to ask the Universe to send me the cards I would see in her reading. I was showed seven cards. They were the first seven cards of her ten-card reading.
This works exceptionally well when you *know your deck*.

## Spirit Readings

My intuitive gifts increased by leaps and bounds once I allowed myself to "pay attention" on a regular basis. What started as just "reading cards" turned into a voyage of sensing people mentally, physically, emotionally, and oddly enough tapping into the Spirit Realm. The latter I was surprised at – even though I have had famous intuitives tell me that this was a gift I had. My biggest block was fear. I had watched so many horror movies in my life that I didn't want anything jumping into me that wouldn't leave!

While on this journey, I invite only the highest vibrations and I trust that I am protected. One day "Spirit" decided to pop in during a reading and I was moved by the experience – and have experienced it ever since.

I have noticed that there is a particular area in my readings that the deceased like to pop up, visit and say "hi" to their loved ones. I usually get fathers – who want to give a clear message. Oddly enough the message is usually the same (I love them, I am proud of them or I am sorry) – so I ALWAYS ask for a confirmation so my client (and I) are confident that I am not pulling multicolored scarves out of my derrière.

That is the defining moment for me. My eyes are often drawn to something specific on a card that I can speak to, or I will "feel" how they died. I sometimes get someone literally "jump into" me. The feeling is always one of overwhelming love that makes me weep – (not my favorite, mind you because I am a girl that loves her make-up and black streaks of mascara running down my face are far from glamorous).

What I can offer, if you feel that this is something you tap into also, is that for me, the deceased usually "pop up" in the same area of a reading – after the tenth card. Learn who your personal "Mother" cards "Father" cards are (again – I have my personal intuitive references, and they may be different than yours). I find that when you are open, Spirit likes to say hello…don't be alarmed. They only go as far as you allow.

# Clairaudiance

When you are doing a reading and a thought or song pops in your head – say it. Often crystal clear messages come through and you may not know what it means. Keep in mind that what you are hearing (or seeing clairvoyantly) is not for you.

# Clairsentiance

Be very aware of your body while in front of your client. For many of us, that is the biggest and best indicator of what is happening with him/her. I had a client who scheduled an appointment with me on a Friday evening for the following Monday. That Monday I woke up with a raging headache. It felt like one of those headaches that you have when you're trying to give up caffeine. I knew it was not mine, because I don't drink a lot of caffeine anymore (which is how I knew it was a caffeine headache). When my client arrived and sat in front of me, the first thing I asked her was, if she had a headache. Her reply, "Yes, I haven't had coffee in three days!"

~

# A Word About Being a Real Intuitive

Once you have shut down your analyzer prior to your readings, do not try to go back and analyze. Often you will get confirmation during a reading and more often you will not get immediate confirmation. The important thing here (and with all intuitive and healing work) is that you do not have an expectation to outcome. *You do not "chase" the reading.*

Often when you do readings a client will say "Yes, that's right," or "oh – I know who that is", etc., but often they sit there quietly and say nothing. Why? Sometimes they are testing you, sometimes they don't know what you are talking about at that moment, and sometimes they are stunned at your accuracy. In any case, do not look for confirmation. During these moments, keep in mind it is not about you. *Real Psychics* are confident in their craft and do not need validation.

~

If you do a number of readings with different clients that provide the same information, – **that is a message for you**. Take heed. In three months, I read two clients and a family friend who won the lottery. Guess what happened next?

# Welcome to My World!

As I have mentioned throughout this workbook, it is imperative for you to connect with your cards in a way that goes beyond traditional approaches. My new clients come to me because their readings are personal – not the standard, "I see the Tower!!!! Something terrible will happen!" – stuff. In fact, I recently pulled the tower when my roof was being replaced. The image on my DruidCraft Tower card was perfect for the day…shingles seem to be flying off the building in the card and I found it comical. If I always subscribed to standard definitions, I would have sat around the house all day in fear.

When you approach your tarot deck as a future best friend, you are not afraid to hear what she has to say. In fact, one of the best things about tarot is that you know whatever "hell" you may be going through, it is temporary…and you get to see the "movie trailers" of your possible future.

While I emphasis the intuitive approach through the relationship development between you and your cards, know that if you are passionate about tarot, there is no need to limit your depth of knowledge. In fact I have read countless books on tarot, have studied with the creator of the Voyager deck James Wanless, enrolled in Tarot Study Schools with Marcus Katz author of Tarosophy, and taken workshops taught by Rachel Pollack and Mary K. Greer. I will continue to develop my knowledge through more books and classes that help me broaden my scope and increase my depth of knowledge.

With the goal of connecting with your deck in mind, I want you to choose from one to three cards a day, or pull three cards that represent the week ahead on Sunday (or whatever day you choose).

If you choose to pull your card at the beginning of the day, that is fine. Some people pull cards at the end of their day in case they see a card they are afraid of. The goal is to do it often enough that you notice patterns. Patterns are best noted based on the consistency and documentation of the experience. For that reason, there is a 12 month blank calendar complete with space to jot down your notes and pages dedicated to a full twelve months of "Personal Insights".

| Sunday | Monday | Tuesday | Wednesday | Thursday | Friday | Saturday |
|--------|--------|---------|-----------|----------|--------|----------|
|        |        |         |           |          |        |          |
|        |        |         |           |          |        |          |
|        |        |         |           |          |        |          |
|        |        |         |           |          |        |          |
|        |        |         |           |          |        |          |

| Sunday | Monday | Tuesday | Wednesday | Thursday | Friday | Saturday |
|--------|--------|---------|-----------|----------|--------|----------|
|        |        |         |           |          |        |          |
|        |        |         |           |          |        |          |
|        |        |         |           |          |        |          |
|        |        |         |           |          |        |          |

| Sunday | Monday | Tuesday | Wednesday | Thursday | Friday | Saturday |
|--------|--------|---------|-----------|----------|--------|----------|
|        |        |         |           |          |        |          |
|        |        |         |           |          |        |          |
|        |        |         |           |          |        |          |
|        |        |         |           |          |        |          |
|        |        |         |           |          |        |          |

| Sunday | Monday | Tuesday | Wednesday | Thursday | Friday | Saturday |
|--------|--------|---------|-----------|----------|--------|----------|
|        |        |         |           |          |        |          |
|        |        |         |           |          |        |          |
|        |        |         |           |          |        |          |
|        |        |         |           |          |        |          |
|        |        |         |           |          |        |          |

| Sunday | Monday | Tuesday | Wednesday | Thursday | Friday | Saturday |
|--------|--------|---------|-----------|----------|--------|----------|
|        |        |         |           |          |        |          |
|        |        |         |           |          |        |          |
|        |        |         |           |          |        |          |
|        |        |         |           |          |        |          |

| Sunday | Monday | Tuesday | Wednesday | Thursday | Friday | Saturday |
|--------|--------|---------|-----------|----------|--------|----------|
|        |        |         |           |          |        |          |
|        |        |         |           |          |        |          |
|        |        |         |           |          |        |          |
|        |        |         |           |          |        |          |

| Sunday | Monday | Tuesday | Wednesday | Thursday | Friday | Saturday |
|--------|--------|---------|-----------|----------|--------|----------|
|        |        |         |           |          |        |          |
|        |        |         |           |          |        |          |
|        |        |         |           |          |        |          |
|        |        |         |           |          |        |          |

| Sunday | Monday | Tuesday | Wednesday | Thursday | Friday | Saturday |
|--------|--------|---------|-----------|----------|--------|----------|
|        |        |         |           |          |        |          |
|        |        |         |           |          |        |          |
|        |        |         |           |          |        |          |
|        |        |         |           |          |        |          |

| Sunday | Monday | Tuesday | Wednesday | Thursday | Friday | Saturday |
|--------|--------|---------|-----------|----------|--------|----------|
|        |        |         |           |          |        |          |
|        |        |         |           |          |        |          |
|        |        |         |           |          |        |          |
|        |        |         |           |          |        |          |

| Sunday | Monday | Tuesday | Wednesday | Thursday | Friday | Saturday |
|--------|--------|---------|-----------|----------|--------|----------|
|        |        |         |           |          |        |          |
|        |        |         |           |          |        |          |
|        |        |         |           |          |        |          |
|        |        |         |           |          |        |          |

| Sunday | Monday | Tuesday | Wednesday | Thursday | Friday | Saturday |
|--------|--------|---------|-----------|----------|--------|----------|
|        |        |         |           |          |        |          |
|        |        |         |           |          |        |          |
|        |        |         |           |          |        |          |
|        |        |         |           |          |        |          |

| Sunday | Monday | Tuesday | Wednesday | Thursday | Friday | Saturday |
|--------|--------|---------|-----------|----------|--------|----------|
|        |        |         |           |          |        |          |
|        |        |         |           |          |        |          |
|        |        |         |           |          |        |          |
|        |        |         |           |          |        |          |

| Sunday | Monday | Tuesday | Wednesday | Thursday | Friday | Saturday |
|--------|--------|---------|-----------|----------|--------|----------|
|        |        |         |           |          |        |          |
|        |        |         |           |          |        |          |
|        |        |         |           |          |        |          |
|        |        |         |           |          |        |          |
|        |        |         |           |          |        |          |

# Insights

In the following pages you will be able to record patterns, insights and other information you deem important as you continue to develop your relationship with this deck.

There are no lines to stay in, no borders to confine you...only blank open space to fill in as you see fit. Open your heart and your mind, spread your wings, and fly!

Remember, your mind is like a parachute...it only functions when it's open!

# Insights

# Insights

# Insights

# Insights

# Insights

# Insights

## Insights

# Insights

# Insights

# Insights

# Insights

# Insights

# Insights

# Insights

# Insights

# Insights

# Insights

# Insights

# Insights

# Insights

# Insights

# Insights

# At the Ready!

## Congratulations!!

If you have done all of these exercises in this book, you are ready to do readings for others. It makes no difference if all the pages are filled – they will be filled in time. You will want to go through most of these exercises with each tarot deck you get. You now understand that all decks are not alike!

## A few words on Professional Tarot Ethics:

- Confidentiality is key: People will trust you with a lot of personal information. Blabber-mouths do not make good friends in the professional tarot community.
- Be Professional: This means look your best, be on time, and do not promise what you can't deliver.
- Do not predict death: It is not up to you to offer that information. That is between God and the intended transitioner.
- Tell the truth: We should all strive to empower our clients. However, if what we see is "bad", it is not "ok" to lie. When you do foresee bad news, do not deliver the news and then request payment, moving on to the next client. The one thing we all know is constant is change. Nothing lasts forever. Look ahead to find the bright spot or lesson for the client.
- Do not read people in the company of their friends (unless someone wants their child read). A reading is a private and personal experience. (I once was approached by a young lady who wanted a reading at my Saturday spot. Her friend immediately took a seat next to her. I politely told the friend that she was not allowed to stay. My client *silently* thanked me profusely.)
- Do not worry about the competition: There are not enough psychics to go around. Each of us offers a different experience. Be confident about what you offer and be supportive of those in our community.

I wish you only the best on your tarot journey! Hold on to your hat….your gifts will continue to unfold, and you come to remember what your purpose is and why you are here.
Safe Travels!
Gina The Tarologist

# Bibliography

Antennucci, Nancy & HJoward, *Psychic Tarot* Melanie Llewllyn 2011

Arynn k Amber & Azrael *Heart of Tarot* Llewlyn 2003

Connolly, Eileen *A New Handbook for the Apprentice Newcastle 1979*

Connolly, Eileen *A New Handbook for the Journeyman Newcastle 1987*

Dale, Cyndi, *The Complete Book of Chakra Healing; Llewellyn 2009*

Dale, Cyndi; *The Advanced Book of Chakra Healing,* The Crossing Press 2005

Gargiulo-Sherman, Johanna; *Guide to the Sacred Rose Tarot;* U.S. Games 1999

Greer Mary k. *21 Ways to read a Tarot Card Llewllyn 2006*

Huggins, Kim *Tarot 101 Llewlyn 2010*

Katz Marcus *Tarosophy Salamander and Sons 2011*

Katz Debra Lynn *You Are Psychic Llewllyn, 2004*

Louis, Anthony; Tarot Plain and Simple; Llellyn, 2000

Made in the USA
Columbia, SC
11 May 2021